DRAGONFLIES

INSECTS IN MY BACKYARD

RYAN JAMES

NORWOOD HOUSE PRESS

Library of Congress Cataloging-in-Publication Data

Names: James, Ryan.
Title: Dragonflies / Ryan James.
Description: Buffalo, NY : Norwood House Press, 2025. | Series: Insects in my backyard | Includes glossary and index.
Identifiers: ISBN 9781684502479 (pbk.) | ISBN 9781684502486 (library bound) | ISBN 9781684502493 (ebook)
Subjects: LCSH: Dragonflies--Juvenile literature.
Classification: LCC QL520.J359 2025 | DDC 595.7'33--dc23

Published in 2025 by
Norwood House Press
2544 Clinton Street
Buffalo, NY 14224

Designer: Ocean Books
Editor: Kim Thompson

Photo credits: Cover, p. 1 aaltair/Shutterstock.com; p. 5 Estuary Pig/Shutterstock.com; p. 6 Parsha/Shutterstock.com; p. 9 Sarulprasanth/Shutterstock.com; p. 10 Bonnie Taylor Barry/Shutterstock.com; p. 11 Jennifer Terp/Shutterstock.com; p. 12 Dr. David Sing/Shutterstock.com; p. 13 Jepp Holcombe/Shutterstock.com; p. 15 Androes Vajar/Shutterstock.com; p. 16 Channon Khutket/Shutterstock.com; p. 17 Helen Cradduck; p. 18 parianto/Shutterstock.com; p. 19 Luke Hercigonja/Shutterstock.com; p. 21 Kesipun/Shutterstock.com

Printed in the United States of America

CPSIA compliance information: Batch #CW25NHP: For further information contact Norwood House Press at 1-800-237-9932.

TABLE OF CONTENTS

WHAT IS A DRAGONFLY?

Dragonflies are fast-flying **insects** you might see in your backyard. They have long bodies and wings that **shimmer** in the sun.

BODY PARTS

Dragonflies have large eyes made up of thousands of tiny **lenses**. Their eyes help them see in all directions.

Dragonflies have two pairs of long, thin wings. Their wings help them fly quickly and **hover** in one place.

A dragonfly's long, slender body helps it move swiftly through the air. Its hard **exoskeleton** provides protection.

TYPES OF DRAGONFLIES

The blue dasher dragonfly is bright blue and green. It can be seen near ponds and streams.

The green darner dragonfly is large with a green body and clear wings. It **migrates** long distances in search of warm weather.

The scarlet skimmer dragonfly is bright red. It loves sunny areas. It often rests on plants near water.

The black saddlebags dragonfly has black spots on its wings that look like saddlebags. It flies through the sky in groups.

DRAGONFLY BEHAVIOR

Dragonflies catch their food while flying. They eat insects like mosquitoes and flies.

Dragonflies rest on plants or rocks near water. They warm their bodies in the sun.

Dragonflies lay eggs in or near water. The **nymphs** that hatch live in the water until they become adults.

WHY ARE DRAGONFLIES IMPORTANT?

Dragonflies eat **pests** like mosquitoes. This makes it more enjoyable to be outside.

Dragonflies are food for birds and fish. They are an important part of the food chain.

Dragonflies need clean water to live and grow. When you see them, you know that the environment is healthy.

GLOSSARY

exoskeleton (EK-soh-skel-uh-tuhn): a hard supporting structure on the outside of the body, as on insects, spiders, and crustaceans

hover (HUHV-ur): to hang suspended in the air

insects (IN-sekts): small animals that have hard outer skeletons instead of backbones and that have three pairs of legs, one or two pairs of wings, and three body sections

lenses (LEN-ziz): clear parts of the eye that focus light on the retina

migrates (MYE-grates): moves from one area to another, especially at certain times of the year or to find food or other resources

nymphs (nimfs): young forms of an insect that become adults by shedding their skin many times

pests (pests): insects or other animals that damage farm crops, that interfere dangerously with human activities, or that annoy people

shimmer (SHIM-ur): to shine with a faint, unsteady light

THINKING QUESTIONS

1. Name three body parts of a dragonfly.
2. How are a blue dasher and a scarlet skimmer alike and different?
3. How do dragonflies grow up?
4. How do you think having an exoskeleton protects dragonflies?
5. Why are dragonflies important?

INDEX

ABOUT THE AUTHOR

Ryan James lives in the western part of North Carolina with his rescue dog Bailey. As a child, he would search for creepy crawlies as he hiked through the forest near his house. When he's not on the hiking or biking trail, he is cheering on his favorite baseball and football teams.